I0181922

THE SKEPTIC'S
HANDBOOK

THE SKEPTIC'S HANDBOOK

MARC BERLIN

A **B** **B** BOOK

A Division of BSF LLC

Copyright © 2012 by Marc Berlin.

All rights reserved. No Part of this book may be reproduced or transmitted in any form or by any means without written permission of the author.

ISBN: 978-0-9859624-2-5

Library of Congress Control Number: 2012913583

Typesetting by www.wordzworth.com

To Mother, and All True Skeptics Everywhere

"Man will never be free until the last king is strangled with the entrails of the last priest."

—DIDEROT

"Do not allow yourselves to be deceived: great minds are skeptical."

—NIETZSCHE

"Stocks have reached what looks like a permanently high plateau."

—IRVING FISHER, PROFESSOR OF ECONOMICS, YALE UNIVERSITY, 1929.

Disclaimer

"The Skeptic's Handbook" is a work of satire by Marc Berlin, and is not intended maliciously. The Author has invented all names and situations in its stories. Any use of real names of any actual persons, living or dead, is entirely accidental and coincidental. In cases where public figures are being satirized, the facts may be totally invented for the sake of parody, humor, or amusement.

Table of Contents

Are Eggs Good For You?   1

Why Are Most Movies Bad?   3

Why Is College So Expensive?   5

When Should I Retire?   6

Are All Families Annoying?   7

Can I Predict When I'll Die?   8

Should I Own Stocks?   9

What's the Best Vacation to Take?   10

Are There Any Jews in Mongolia?   11

Are There Any Mongols in Israel?   12

Did Lincoln Own Slaves?   13

Was George Washington Funny?   14

Is Bill Gates Happy?   15

What's the 'Military Industrial Complex'?   16

Are Jerks Born That Way?   18

Who was Stanley Obama?   19

Are Banks Honest?   20

Do I Have To Pay Income Taxes?   21

How Many Homes Does Mitt Romney Own?   22

Can I Collect Disability?   23

Is a New Roof Deductible?   24

How Rich is Donald Trump?   25

Are Movie Reviews Accurate?   26

What is Nepotism?   27

What Does the Supreme Court Do?   28

What's the Longest Running TV Show in History?   29
Why Are Soap Operas So Popular?   30
What's the Worst Country in the World?   31
Can Anyone Be a Celebrity?   32
Can I Get Cancer From My Cat?   33
Is Broccoli Really Good For You?   34
Where do Aliens Come From?   35
Is Pro Football Dangerous?   36
Why is Health Insurance So Expensive?   38
What are the Seven Wonders of the Modern World?   40
Who are the Mormons?   41
Who are the Boy Scouts?   42
Did Shakespeare Write His Own Plays?   43
Is The Law Still a Good Profession?   44
Who Painted 'American Gothic'?   45
What is Homophobia?   47
What Did Nietzsche Believe?   48
What Does Passover Celebrate?   50
What Was the Longest Tennis Match in History?   51
Is Time Travel Possible?   52
How Common is Cheating?   53
Is Nuclear War Likely?   55
What Do Women Find Attractive?   57
What's the Worst City in America?   59
What's the 'Tobacco Lobby'?   61
What's the 'Gun Lobby'?   62
Who Invented the Hammer?   63
What's the Worst Food to Eat?   64

How Accurate is the U.S. Unemployment Rate?	66
Where Does Queen Elizabeth Live?	67
Who Was the 'Fifth Beatle'?	69
Is There Life After Death?	71
How Important is a Good Resume?	72
Why is There So Much Divorce?	74
Is Smoking in Bed Dangerous?	75
Who was the Best President?	77
What is an App?	79
Is Mideast Peace Possible?	80
How is Cricket Played?	81

Are Eggs Good For You?

In the last several years, eggs have been vilified as being an extremely harmful food, causing everything from heart disease and stroke, to the rise in teen pregnancies and global warming. While these accusations are for the most part true, eggs remain an excellent source of many essential nutrients which the human body desperately needs, and which should thus be part of any daily diet. For example, in addition to being the only food that contains the full complement of amino acids, eggs are also a good source of protein and fat, which help absorb fat-soluble vitamins like A, B, C and G. Another fallacy concerns what parts of an egg are safe to eat. Although for centuries people believed only the yoke and white part were acceptable to ingest, laboratory tests have proven that the *hard exterior shell* of the egg is also highly edible, as well as, surprisingly, the most nutritious. "Eggs have been given a bum rap in recent years," Dr. Myron Sauerkraut, head of the Northeast New Jersey Egg Council says. "They sort of became the Al Capone of foods, if you will. The fact is, you can't eat *too many* eggs. I myself eat sixteen a day. I'd eat even more if I had time, but I don't." Regarding the high cholesterol content of eggs, about 200 mg each, Sauerkraut says this, too, should be of little concern to the average person. "Humans can ingest an amazing amount of choles-

1

terol, fat, even poisons, without suffering any ill effects whatsoever," he contends. "In my experience as a cardiac surgeon in a very busy private practice, problems only arise if you overdo it, or if you eat while driving or having sex, which is probably true about *almost anything*."

Why Are Most Movies Bad?

Movies are logistical nightmares, requiring hundreds of people to produce, including writers, directors and crew, as well as – behind the scenes – executives, chauffeurs, and private masseuses. All of this makes them very expensive endeavors, especially the kind produced in Hollywood starring high-priced glamorous celebrities. Since the early days of Hollywood, the big movie studios have always consciously *dumbed-down* their 'product' in order to attract the widest *audience* possible – and hopefully earn back their considerable investment in the shortest *time* possible. This scenario makes for poorly conceptualized projects, shoddily produced, that most *eight year olds* would reject. Theoretically, *anyone* can make a movie – all it takes is a good digital camera, two or three talented actors, and a small, dedicated crew willing to work for a free ham sandwich and a shabby motel room, usually with some dope thrown in. A good script on the other hand, meaning one with a well-written *substantive plot*, is for a variety of reasons exceedingly rare. Young people today, some a few weeks out of college or film school, are making movies on the flimsiest of shoestring budgets, saturating the market with profoundly incoherent films that only a tiny handful of people will ever have time to watch anyway. Amazingly, despite all of this, most movies

3

are still considerably better than the unmitigated rubbish shown on TV.

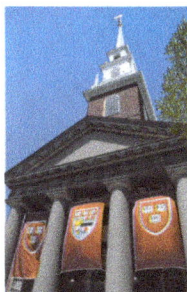

Why Is College So Expensive?

The current average cost of one year at a private college in the U.S. is approximately $48,000, or $15,000 at a public one. This price doesn't include spring breaks in Florida, or cognition-enhancing recreational drugs. College is expensive because everyone wants to go there, even kids from poor households whose parents can't afford it and are willing to go deep into debt to send their children to an institution merely because it has ivy all over it. If everyone wanted to go to *Cleveland*, that would be expensive too. Because of the law of supply and demand, starting in the late 1990's college administrators realized there was virtually no limit to how much they could charge for tuition, and that the applicant pool was literally bottomless. Professors soon wanted in on the action too, and began demanding, and getting, sky high salaries approaching Brad Pitt's payday. One way for a young person to avoid college costs is to drop out soon after they matriculate, like Bill Gates. (See: *"Is Bill Gates Happy?"*)

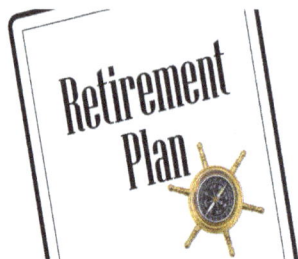

When Should I Retire?

Almost all financial planners agree: it's never too early to start saving for retirement. Regular contributions to a well-diversified IRA along with monthly, even daily, consultations with a certified financial planner or experienced palm-reader can mean the difference between a comfortable retirement in a gated community in Florida, and a grimy sub-basement studio in Newark. "A general rule of thumb is, by the time you retire you should have more money in the bank than your height in inches divided by your weight in grams multiplied by 134," says Nadine Kidneystone, a certified financial planner based in Tucson, Arizona. "Anything less than that and you're probably headed straight for that stuffy attic room at your daughter's house." She adds: "Retiring *too early* isn't advisable either. You'll *wake up* too early and find yourself wandering around the house for half a day. So be very careful, and plan accordingly."

Are *All* Families Annoying?

While the overwhelming majority of families are completely benign, meaning kind, loving and supportive, some families can be exactly the opposite: highly critical, wildly *un*support-ive, and unforgiving – meaning bad and annoying, possibly even detrimental to your health. Typically, annoying families are most annoying when they've gathered together for some annual ritual, such as Christmas, Thanksgiving, or Kwanza, and everyone is seated at the same big dinner table where age-old resentments and petty grievances quickly bubble to the surface, often leading to embarrassing squabbles, endless bickering, food fights, and stress. The best way to avoid annoying families is to move as far away as possible as soon as possible, preferably to another city or state. (But *not* San Bernardino. See: *"What's the Worst City in America?"*) Or even to another *country* like Myanmar (formerly Burma) or the Central African Republic. If moving isn't practical, at minimum an unlisted phone number, or caller ID, should be seriously considered.

Can I Predict When I'll Die?

The average person, meaning in the U.S. someone living in Toledo, Ohio making $53,300 per year with 2.2 kids, has no idea at all when they'll die, unless they're contemplating suicide and have a note ready. Actuaries, the people who work for big insurance companies and are paid to predict mortality rates, know *precisely* when you'll die, sometimes to the hour, but are sworn to secrecy lest everyone becomes profoundly depressed all at once, causing GDP to plummet and society to implode. As Benjamin Franklin once famously said, "A penny saved is a penny earned." He also, much less famously, said, "You can never have enough insurance."

Should I Own Stocks?

Many of the Pilgrims who survived the difficult trans-Atlantic voyage from England to America were in a sour mood, and had to be taught a quick lesson if they stepped out of line. For this reason, soon after they landed at Plymouth Rock the Pilgrims invented *stocks* – a pair of wooden boards between which a criminal would be placed, and partially immobilized, for the purpose of exposing the miscreant to public humiliation and ridicule. The criminal was placed in a stock, usually in the town square, doused with vegetable oil or some similar brand of salad dressing, then laughed at continuously for an hour and a half by their neighbors and *former* friends. Hence the term 'laughingstock'. In *Mass. Bay Colony v. Epstein*, the stock was eventually deemed unconstitutional as being cruel and unusual and was quickly replaced by the ducking stool, followed by the garrote, burning at the stake, and finally the firing squad and electrocution. There's no need for anyone in modern times to own stocks, unless their kids are misbehaving.

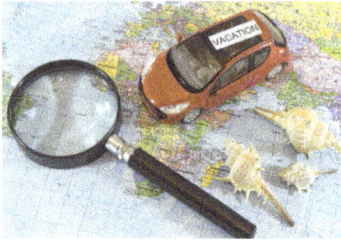

What's the Best Vacation to Take?

A once-a-year two-week vacation should always be on everyone's list of things to do. Unfortunately, as people's lives become increasingly hectic, vacations are becoming harder to take. According to *Modern Mistress* Magazine, the best getaway value is a two-week all-inclusive stay in Tahiti, preferably with a young, physically attractive partner who enjoys sleeping, and having wild sex, in a thatched hut by the ocean. Although a plane ride to Tahiti can be long and expensive, its remoteness makes Tahiti unusually secure. Also, the people there are friendly and almost everyone speaks Tahitian. The *worst* vacation to take is a tie: between a week in Damascus, Syria, where open warfare has broken out between anti-government revolutionaries and the despotic regime of Bashar al-Assad, and a three-week safari in Zimbabwe, where roving packs of armed teenaged gangs regularly assault tourists at will.

Are There Any Jews in Mongolia?

The Jewish population of Mongolia is 4, all of them members of the Tensingstein family who reside in a tent, or *yurt*, at the end of Lop Nor Avenue. The patriarch of the family is Yehuda, 43, who makes his living repairing yurts, or tents, and by selling recycled ones. He and his wife, Sarah, have two young children who plan to attend Yeshiva, probably in 11 years when it's estimated it'll be fully operational. The family owns no TV or car, but each carries an i-phone provided by the Mongol government. Anyone wishing to contact them may do so at the following number: 976-4.

Are There Any Mongols in Israel?

No.

Did Lincoln Own Slaves?

Abraham Lincoln, the 16th President of the United States and signer of the Emancipation Proclamation, secretly owned a small family of black slaves, the Washingtons, who lived in the basement of the White House. Little is known about them, or why President Lincoln kept them there, but historians have speculated that Lincoln was profoundly bored and very lonely, especially during the depths of the Civil War, and enjoyed spying on the Washingtons through a secret one-way mirror as they whiled away the hours singing spirituals and darning clothes for Union troops. He also liked their home-style cooking and ready humor. In 1864, Lincoln tried to free the Washingtons, but the patriarch of the family, *Wishy*, insisted their proper place was the White House basement, where he, and then his many descendants, remained until 1981.

Was George Washington Funny?

The first president and father of our country, George Washington was described by close acquaintances, and even Redcoats, as being extremely funny, sometimes hysterically so. Historian Jack E. Mason, author of *"Washington: The First Laugh"*, says General Washington was always joking around with his men during the Revolutionary War, especially under difficult circumstances. "Either crossing his fingers on the Delaware, showing up half-naked for tedious portrait sessions, or tossing cherry bombs from his horse, humor was clearly an outlet for him," Mason says. "As president, Washington found John Adams unfunny and repetitive, 'a downright bore.' In his memoirs, Washington called Jefferson 'a humorless toad...always scribbling, but no jokes. Even a bad one woulde be welcome.'" Washington was seriously considering a career as a humorist and comic, before history, and his wife Martha, intervened, and he was forced to jettison the idea.

Is Bill Gates Happy?

Bill Gates, philanthropist, co-founder of Microsoft and the 2nd richest man in the world with an estimated personal worth of close to $60 billion, has been known by friends and co-workers to be testy, agitated, ironic, sullen and sometimes even impish, but never really happy. He's also been known to be absent-minded, folksy, nervous, overpowering, as well as vain and cranky. In a 2005 interview with *Billionaire* magazine, Gates admitted that having sixty billion dollars is great, even wonderful at times, and that having *more* than sixty billion, a lot more, maybe even as much as a hundred billion, would be fantastic and obviously stupendous. Although sixty billion dollars, a 30,000 square foot lakeside mansion and a fleet of private jets are all wonderful to have, Gates has explicitly stated that the *most* important things in his life are his wife Melinda and their three children – Jennifer, Katharine, and Starting. In *addition* to the sixty billion.

What's the 'Military Industrial Complex'?

The military industrial complex is an archipelago of manufacturing and research companies doing highly profitable defense-related work for the U.S. Government. Located strategically throughout America and overseas, the unstated purpose of the Complex is to loudly complain about defense cutbacks. By extension it vigorously warns of the potential danger to America's security whenever a member of Congress or the media suggests saving billions of wasted taxpayer dollars by, for example, not purchasing the B-2 and C-17 Bombers, the V-2 Osprey, or seven hundred dollar toilet seats for the P-3 aircraft. Thousands of companies large and small covering a variety of industries are represented in the Complex, including Halliburton, Northrup-Grumman, Lockheed-Martin, Boeing, Raytheon, and General Electric, to name only a few. The unstated beauty of the Military Industrial Complex is that from the outset, during and just after the Second World War, and then beyond, its member corporations attempted *with great success* to locate their operations in most if not all of the fifty states, employing millions of workers and thereby guaranteeing the ears of Congress whenever and wherever its financial interests were perceived to be under attack. Below, is a partial list of Defense Department weapons systems that were the victims of cost overruns and technical problems during the last 20 years:

- A-10 Warthog Aircraft
- Ballistic Missile Defense
- C-130J Transport Aircraft
- Crusader Howitzer
- Joint Strike Fighter Aircraft
- B-1 Bomber
- Black Hawk Helicopter
- Comanche Helicopter
- Stryker Interim Armored Vehicle
- Predator Unmanned Aerial Vehicle (Drone)

Are Jerks Born That Way?

Jerks are highly annoying people who make life consistently miserable for those around them. Overwhelmingly male, jerks can be found in a variety of places, including business meetings, family reunions, and movie lines, just to name a few. Characterized by extreme arrogance, social immaturity and pathological self-obsession, jerks are especially common in the workplace, where very often they have managerial positions and can't be avoided. According to Dr. Arnold Millstein, a psychiatrist in Bethesda, Maryland, being a jerk is an inborn personality trait, usually inherited from the father. "If the father is an arrogant mannerless jackass, most likely at least *one* of his male offspring will be one too. It's almost impossible to change someone's spots, if you will." Millstein adds: "The good news is, new therapies are being developed to help alleviate the stress and emotional toll of someone nearby being a jerk. Genetic profiling will no doubt help too. For these reasons, victims of this dreaded condition can and should remain extremely hopeful."

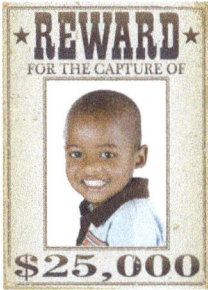

Who was Stanley Obama?

Contrary to many heavy biographies by a variety of highly regarded authors, Stanley Obama was *not* Barack Obama's mother. Stanley was the name of Obama's identical twin brother, a child prodigy able to recite Shakespeare backwards and play the piano underwater. Unfortunately, Stanley was also a juvenile delinquent, who by the age of ten had already robbed several Honolulu savings banks and pet stores. Horrified and embarrassed by Stanley's criminal exploits, the family put the young boy up for adoption. Initially, there were no takers. Ultimately, Stanley was sent to Indonesia where he lived until his death, from senile dementia, at the age of 15. In an effort to explain the young man's disappearance, Barack Obama's mother, *Jerry*, took Stanley's name for herself.

Are Banks Honest?

The answer to this oft-posed question is simple: no. Banks are in the business of making a profit, not holding your money for a while, like your grandmother or top dresser drawer, until you need it. To fill their increasingly insatiable desire for profits *from any source*, banks are now levying hefty fees for items that were once free. For example, many large banks now charge customers a fee if their feet are wet when they enter the bank. Others charge a small fee if you don't smile at the teller, or if you fail to wave at the manager when he arrives at eleven o'clock. One person sued his bank after it debited his account $500 for having *too* much money in it, and the safe broke. Ultimately, if a customer feels he is being mistreated, he can always take his business elsewhere. But banks often share information with other banks about disloyal customers, and the practice is frowned upon.

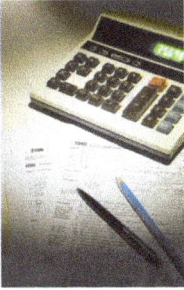

Do I Have To Pay Income Taxes?

Like those two other great American pastimes, baseball and the weather, Americans love to talk to about taxes. If there was no income tax, there'd be nothing for Americans to complain about. Most conservatives and rich people, which are generally the same thing, hate paying taxes, especially the dreaded estate or 'death' tax, as it leaves them with less money to buy more yachts and third and fourth homes with. (See: *"How Many Homes Does Mitt Romney Own?"*) Anyone who earns money is required to file an income tax return and, presumably, pay the tax owed. Depending on how clever your tax lawyer is, and/or how politically well-connected you are, the penalties for not doing so can be severe. As a rule, poor people pay the most tax as a percentage of their total income, yet ironically they complain the least.

How Many Homes Does Mitt Romney Own?

Willard "Mitt" Romney, the former Governor of Massachu-setts and the presumed Republican candidate for president in 2012, owns nine homes in eleven different states. For this reason, he could be considered a resident of no *one* state. Also for this reason, some liberals have argued Romney *isn't even a U.S. citizen.* In addition to his many homes, Romney also owns sixteen cars, fourteen boats, nineteen horses, two racetracks, and a delicatessen in Provo, Utah he acquired while CEO of Bain Capital in Boston, which he headed before taking over The Olympics and becoming Governor. With a personal net worth estimated at over $250 million, most of it deposited in numbered Cayman Island and Swiss bank accounts, Romney can afford to live almost anywhere, and for a brief period in 2005 owned the entire eleventh floor of the Ritz Carlton Hotel in Boston. More recently, Romney and his wife, Ann, acquired title to a private island in the Bahamas, as well as a "small" planet in the constellation Virgo.

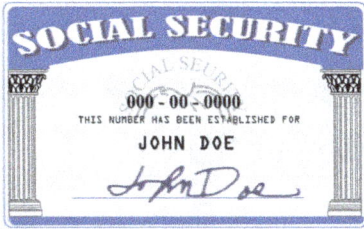

Can I Collect Disability?

Disability (SSDI) is an insurance program run by the U.S. government as part of Social Security. If you become disabled, either physically or mentally, you can collect a monthly payment, the amount of which depends on how much money you made while working. In poor economic times, a few bad apples will try to collect disability instead of working. The problem is, you have to *prove* you're actually disabled to collect. People will often go to almost any length to prove they're disabled, and thus qualify. One man pretended he was a donkey; another cut his own arms and legs off then claimed he was a basketball. (Both claims were denied.) Many Americans are truly disabled, and rely on the program to pay for food and other basic necessities – which is why rich people, Republicans particularly, tend to hate it.

Is a New Roof Deductible?

A new roof for your home may, or may not be, deductible on your income tax return. A lot depends on whom you speak to. "Theoretically, *everything* is deductible, assuming the IRS doesn't find out about it," Marv Winkman, a CPA with Winkman and Hyde in Bethesda, Maryland, says. "If the IRS finds out about it, then most likely they'll deny it and you're screwed." But how would they find out about it? "They'd find out about it if two guys in dark suits visited your home as part of an audit. They'd notice your new roof, then immediately take out an electron microscope and look much more closely at your return to see if you tried to deduct it." Winkman adds: "On the other hand, if you tried to deduct, say, a motor-yacht you keep in Antigua, you'd have a much better chance because they probably wouldn't see it. It's the old adage: Out of sight, out of mind. From personal experience, at the end of the day it's all a giant crapshoot."

How Rich is Donald Trump?

Donald Trump is a wealthy real estate investor based in New York City. Starting with a portfolio of mainly middle class housing units inherited from his father, Fred, Trump went on to amass a small empire consisting of luxury apartment buildings, hotels, and casinos, including The Trump Tower in New York City and The Taj Mahal, a casino in Atlantic City. Through a shrewd combination of good timing, unabashed self-promotion, and inherited family wealth, as well as a mane of carefully-coiffed flowing blond hair, Trump has built a personal fortune variously estimated at anywhere from a few hundred million dollars to several billion, depending on the day of the week. Now married to his third wife, Melania, 'The Donald' has several attractive children who appear regularly on his TV show, "You're *Fired!*" Much like Mitt Romney, another famous wealthy American with a successful father and way too much free time on his hands, Trump makes occasional ill-advised, highly embarrassing forays into politics, usually with disastrous results. Trump's serial failures at politics are largely due to the fact that he's reportedly terrified of germs, including his own, and hates to shake hands. He once admitted to a reporter that the secret to his success is clearly his deal-making ability, plus his hair, which he keeps in a jar next to his bed.

Are Movie Reviews Accurate?

It's a widely-know but well-kept secret in Hollywood, that movie reviews have little effect on whether a film is successful or not. In fact, scientists at the Roy Rogers School of Cinema Studies at USC have proven an almost exact *inverse* correlation between the reviews a film garners, and how much box office it takes in. As an example, numerous critics condemned the sci-fi action movie *"The Hunger Games"* as very poorly written as well as technically inept. Yet, the picture made billions worldwide; as of 2012, four sequels are planned. "Art" films, better-made movies and thus ones that tend to get positive reviews, are usually shunned by audiences, especially *male teens* and young girls who make up most of the movie-going audience, and who can't read anyway. For this reason, movie studios will often pay a 'respected' reviewer to write a harshly negative review, almost guaranteeing a film will be financially successful. Senate hearings have been scheduled about this nefarious practice, but no legislation, as yet, has been enacted.

What is Nepotism?

Nepotism, from the Latin word n*epos*, or nephew, is a cult-like religion which originated in the early Middle Ages, mostly in Europe. During that period, adherents to the cult, called *Nepotists*, usually nobles or other rich landowners, would round up, then ritually murder, any male under twenty-five, so that the noble's immediate offspring (or close relatives) would be guaranteed jobs when they came of age. Nepotism gradually lost favor in Europe, but re-emerged two centuries later, especially in the Middle East where democratic rule, or even the rule of law, was still virtually unknown. In the West, Nepotism became popular again in late 20th century America, reaching its zenith (some would say nadir) in a Supreme Court case known as *Bush v. Gore*, in which George W. Bush, an extremely well-connected but relatively inexperienced baseball team owner whose father had already been president, was *appointed* president despite his obvious lack of qualifications and tendency to smirk.

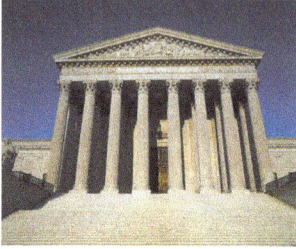

What Does the Supreme Court Do?

The U.S. Supreme Court consists of nine old people, called *justices*. The justices, five Republicans and four Democrats, decide difficult, arcane cases that lower courts have decided are too confusing, or simply too tedious, to handle. Each case consists of oral arguments before the full court, followed by a lengthy, convoluted 500-page 'majority' decision, or *opinion*, usually characterized by numerous double and triple negatives and which few people in the world understand. By tradition, all court justices had to be alumni of the venerable Harvard Law School, although in recent years this requirement has been loosened so that now some come from Yale, but only a few. The most famous Supreme Court case is *Brown v. The Board of Education of Topeka Kansas*. To this day, no one knows what this case means or why the court decided to hear it, except that it probably sounded too good for the justices to pass up. Some people have criticized the court for being too activist; others for wearing robes and slippers to work.

What's the Longest Running TV Show in History?

The longest-running episodic TV show in network history is generally considered to be *Gunsmoke*, an hour-long black and white, and then color Western which ran for 20 years on CBS. Starring James Arness as U.S. Marshal Matt Dillon, each episode would usually show Dillon talking to his romantic interest and saloonkeeper, Miss Kitty, or drinking beer with his twangy sidekick, Festus, and thus not noticing that the Dodge City bank was being robbed. Even though he's highly respected by the townsfolk and hates violence, in almost every episode Dillon is forced to shoot to death three or four people before the end of each show. The longest-running *non-network* program in TV history is "Sid's Silo", a morning show produced by KORN-TV in Omaha Nebraska. This ten-minute program, mostly about grain and livestock prices, but also the daily likelihood of a Russian nuclear attack against the ICBM installation at Warren Air Force Base, has been on the air continuously for 62 years.

Why Are Soap Operas So Popular?

Soap operas, so-called because they were originally sponsored by companies selling soap or detergent, have been on TV for generations. Despite their overall themelessness, tedious predictability and byzantine incoherent plots and storylines that make wallpaper look interesting by comparison, stay-at-home moms and others with average or *below average* intelligence find soaps mesmerizing. These loyal viewers would rather jump in front of a speeding subway train or drink strychnine than miss even a single episode. Despite their obvious drawbacks, many fans find the characters' lives in soaps more real and interesting than their own, to the point where a number have been involuntarily committed to state mental hospitals where they spend endless hours in front of a TV – watching their favorite soap opera.

What's the Worst Country in the World?

The worst country in the world *used* to be *Paraguay*, where ex-Nazis would flee to, along with a suitcase stuffed with cash, in order to set up a new life for themselves and their families far from Nuremburg. Beginning in 2001, however, a little known sultanate, called *Badmintonia*, had easily moved into first place as worst place. The country is actually a tiny coral atoll, three football fields in length, 2,200 nautical miles northeast of Tasmania. It has no taxes, no schools, and no public restrooms. In Badmintonia, it's illegal *not* to carry an AK-47, and a capital offense to listen to the radio after three p.m. Being a woman, asking a question, as well as whispering in public are also highly illegal, and anyone not a native Badmintonian is immediately imprisoned after passing through airport customs. The country has been compared to the State of Texas, which has many similar laws and customs.

Can *Anyone* Be a Celebrity?

At one time or another, everyone dreams of being a celebrity. But only a microscopic sliver of the population can actually become one. Celebrity-dom is essentially a closed shop, and unless your father is the head of a movie studio, or you've committed a heinous crime like defrauding a hedge fund or shooting fifty people in a shopping mall, it's very difficult to become a celebrity. In addition to making a nauseating amount of money in their chosen fields in a relatively short amount of time, celebrities can earn even more income by *lecturing*, sometimes for as much as $100,000 per appearance, or by doing commercials for sleazy insurance companies or fly-by-night reverse mortgage outfits. Despite the obvious perks that come with being a celebrity, celebrities eventually learn that money and fame, even unlimited access to hordes of highly attractive young women, is not necessarily a recipe for perpetual bliss. Additionally, celebrities carry the added burden of having to fend off swarms of annoying paparazzi, or owning big cars that are hard to park.

Can I Get Cancer From My Cat?

According to the American Cancer Society, cat-to-human cancer is not unknown, with more than a few cases being reported, mostly in sub-Sahara Africa, Brazil, and The Yukon. Generally, however, carcinogenic felines are exceedingly rare. The disease is usually transmitted gradually, after years of petting and licking, *then doing the same with your cat,* as well as through repeated handling of the animal's waste box and partially-eaten cat treats. Mice, squirrels and other rodents that commonly interact with domesticated cats have also been known to carry the disease, transferring it to a human host through the air while scooting across an open basement floor or along a room's wainscoting.

Is Broccoli Really Good For You?

A member of the cabbage family, broccoli is considered by doctors and nutritionists to be one of the best foods a person can eat. High in dietary fiber, thiamine and vitamin C, broccoli has been known to be an effective weapon against cancer, arthritis, whooping cough and malaria. Unfortunately, despite ranking high on the list of healthy foods, *children* hate broccoli because of its strange flowery appearance, as well as its tendency to become mushy if overcooked. President George H.W. Bush once casually admitted that *he* hated broccoli too, a statement that alienated many Americans who enjoy it, and may have cost him the 1992 election against Bill Clinton, especially in Iowa. The most common type of broccoli is Calabrese, named for the Calabria region in Italy. Contrary to popular belief, broccoli was not invented (or even grown) by Albert "Cubby" Broccoli, an American film producer responsible for many of the James Bond movies, including *The Spy Who Loved Me* and *Octopussy*.

Where do Aliens Come From?

Scientists have been studying aliens for hundreds of years, probably since the beginning of recorded history. Despite this, they still don't know where aliens come from. One theory, developed by the U.S. Government as part of their highly classified *"Wetback"* program, is that aliens come from a small town in Mexico just north of Veracruz called *Chilipeppa*, and also from a Honduran banana plantation much farther south, where local wages are so low and the plumbing so poor that the place empties out every couple of days. In 2004, a vast array of extra large satellite dishes was set up on the southern border of the U.S. along the Rio Grande in an attempt to intercept an actual alien ship as it tried to cross the border. Until one actually does, it's all a big guess.

Is Pro Football Dangerous?

Compared to some other highly dangerous professions, pro football is relatively safe. Still, pro football as played in the NFL is an extremely rough contact sport. Pro football players, some weighing as much as a light pickup truck, are required to hit each other as hard as possible, usually in the head, neck or back, often with the sole purpose of causing serious bodily harm. As a result, numerous cases of traumatic brain injury have been reported, many of which don't manifest themselves until much later, usually well after the player has retired. Below, is a list of professions in their order of dangerousness:

1   U.S. Army Ranger
2   U.S. Navy SEAL
3   Mine clearer
4   Drug Enforcement Officer (Ciudad Juarez, Mexico)
5   Pro Football Player

In recent years, a number of ex-NFL players have come forward complaining of a wide variety of cognitive and physical impairments, decades after retiring from the game. Despite these troubling stories, most players have enjoyed successful, injury-free careers without suffering any ill-effects at all. "I played pro ball for eight years, and as far as I know

I'm perfectly OK," one former NFL defensive lineman says. "I wake up, make breakfast, and liver on the corncob plainly belfry inside mouse." A class-action lawsuit against the league is now being contemplated by over a hundred former players, or their survivors.

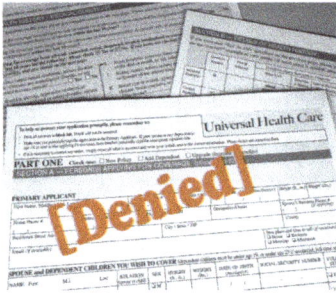

Why is Health Insurance So Expensive?

Health insurance premiums in the U.S. have skyrocketed in recent years, making access to health care increasingly difficult, not only for the poor and working poor, but also for many Americans who consider themselves middle and even upper middle class. One reason for the explosive rise in premiums is the increasingly high cost of hospital and physician care. Below, is a partial list of costs to deliver medical care at a typical private hospital in the U.S.:

- Scalpel - $3400.
- Fluids bag - $2570.
- Reclinable hospital bed - $56,400
- Kleenex - $560.
- Syringe (disposable) - $890.
- Nightgown - $1625.

Along with hospital costs, the price of physician care has soared as well, far outpacing inflation. Because of the longer hours associated with the increasing burden of preparing insurance paperwork, many physicians have quit the profession altogether. "I have expenses too, tons of them," one internist in private practice in San Francisco explains. "To send both my son and daughter to excellent prestigious colleges – that's $53,000 per year, *per kid*. My wife wants a midwinter week in St. Barts? – bam, that's seven grand. Second and third vacation homes, one in the mountains, the other by the beach and all the expenses that go with it? At the end of the day it all adds up and I have to pay for it somehow. Otherwise, I'm screwed."

What are the Seven Wonders of the Modern World?

According to *Webster's New World Wonders Dictionary*, the following are the *official* Seven Wonders of the Modern World:

- George W. Bush was elected President.
- George W. Bush was *re*-elected President.
- Baseball is America's favorite pastime.
- Many People Watch Golf on TV.
- Many People Watch Auto Racing on TV.
- Millions Still Smoke Cigarettes.
- Trickle-Down Economics Remains a Viable Theory.

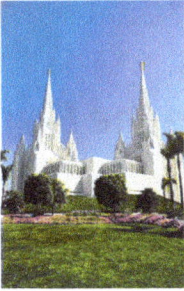

Who are the Mormons?

The Mormons, most of whom live in the U.S. state of Utah and believe in the Book of Mormon and the Christian Bible, are the principal branch of the *Latter Day Saint Movement*. Variously described as a religion, a cult, and a 501(c) (3) charitable organization, Mormonism was founded around 1820 in upstate New York by Joseph Smith, who along with his brother Al invented the cherry cough drop. Mormons believe in strong family values, a sense of community, and refraining from using alcohol (but not *rubbing* alcohol). Although *polygamy*, the taking of multiple wives, is technically illegal and frowned upon by the Church, an un-surprisingly large number of Mormon men continue to flaunt the law, sometimes marrying hundreds, or even thousands of attractive women at the same time, then living together in perpetual bliss as one big gigantic family in the same house, many of them 50-bathroom palaces on the hilly outskirts of Salt Lake City. In recent years, some Mormon women have rebelled against this practice, and are now demanding and obtaining similar rights for themselves, going so far as taking multiple husbands, a taboo practice in itself known as *husbandry*.

Who are the Boy Scouts?

The Boy Scouts of America (B.S.A.) is a youth organization for boys, and adult volunteers, with millions of members worldwide. With its motto of "Be prepared", the goal of the Boy Scouts is to teach young men to be responsible, independent citizens, and to instill a sense of trustworthiness, good citizenship, honor, compassion, courage, and kindred spirits, along with patriotism and self-reliance, mainly by developing outdoor survival skills such as knot-making and homophobia. (See: *What is Homophobia?*) Founded in the 1920's by the newspaper publisher W.D. Boyce, the Scouts is generally limited to boys aged 11 to 18 under six feet tall. Starting in the 1990's, the Boy Scouts became the target of a series of embarrassing lawsuits, generally over a variety of restrictive admission policies. In *Gordian v. Boy Scouts of America*, the Scouts were accused of making knots too difficult to untie. *In Girl Scouts v. Boy Scouts*, The Girl Scouts of America sued the Boy Scouts for barring membership to three girls who had already proven they could build a small campfire, and wear badges, as well as boys could. In 2004, in *Brownies v. Cub Scouts*, the Brownies, another sister organization limited to girls under four feet, sued the Cub Scouts for not allowing membership to girls under four feet.

Did Shakespeare Write His Own Plays?

William Shakespeare, widely considered to be the greatest dramatist and writer in history, most likely wrote very few, *if any*, of his plays. Scholars agree that Shakespeare, or 'The Bard' as he was known, was far too busy acting in other people's dramas, gardening in his back yard, or taking care of his two daughters, Susanna and Judith, to have the spare time needed to write the 32 plays and 158 sonnets he's credited with. Actually, very little is known about Shakespeare's personal life. Although he married Anne Hathaway in 1582, scholars suspect Shakespeare may have had many early love affairs, and later mistresses, most of whom were probably local wenches and harlots from in and around the hamlet of Stratford-upon-Avon, his hometown, and whom he no doubt used as the basis of characters in the few plays he *did* have time to write, including *"Where There's a Willy"* (1599), and *"Anne Hath a Way" (1605)*. Shakespeare was a great actor and ladies' man, but an abject failure as a businessman, and was often forced to resort to other modes of work, including being a waiter and writing advertising copy, to make ends meet. He died in 1616, after falling off his beloved horse, Frank.

Is The Law Still a Good Profession?

Despite its long history as a prestigious, highly lucrative calling, making sacks of money as an attorney is no longer guaranteed. The gauntlet of becoming a lawyer has always been, and continues to be, a difficult time-consuming one, and also increasingly expensive. Prospective lawyers must, first, submit to a ten-hour three-day standardized intelligence test known as the LSAT, followed by three highly stressful as well as often very lonely years at an accredited law school, many costing well over $50,000 per year. Legal jobs during and even *after* law school are few, and becoming increasingly hard to obtain, especially without extensive family connections – and even then involve long, tedious hours doing research in a firm's musty fluorescent-lit law library for little or no pay, with little chance for meaningful advancement. At the end of the day, most legal jobs are extremely boring, usually requiring soul-draining drudgery such as preparing endless reams of mind-numbing paperwork better suited to a rhesus monkey, filing stacks of frivolous lawsuits, or chasing ambulances. Despite these sobering warnings, many young people still desperately crave a life in the law, and will do almost anything, including *running over their own grandmother with an armored personnel carrier,* to gain a spot at an accredited law school.

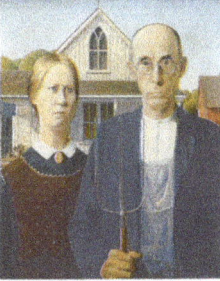

Art (c) Figge Art Museum, successors to the Estate of

Nan Wood Graham/Licensed by VAGA, New York, NY

Who Painted 'American Gothic'?

One of the most familiar as well as iconic American paintings in history, 'American Gothic' was painted in 1930 by *Grant Wood*. Using his sister, Nan, and his dentist, Byron McKeeby, as models, Wood created a memorable, faintly humorous tableau, brimming with metaphor and complexity, showing a farmer holding a pitchfork as he stands, almost befuddled, next to his equally befuddled daughter (and not his wife as many people believe). The structure in the background of the painting, a simple white farmhouse Wood found in Eldon, Iowa, echoes the three prongs of the pitchfork, as well as the farmer's face. Using a style called *regionalism,* many critics assumed Wood's painting was meant as a satire of small town life in America, particularly rural America. This analysis was only partly correct. The painting is clearly meant to be a satire of big city *art critics,* who, predictably at first, dismissed Wood's painting as an amusing curiosity, a trifle not worthy to hang anywhere let alone in a museum, and who only, much later, saw it being on a par with Michelangelo's *Sistine Chapel,* Leonardo's *Mona Lisa,* and Munch's *The Scream,* plus other great works of western art. The picture made a brief appearance in several movies and TV shows, including *The Rocky Horror Picture Show* and *Dr. Who,* and also in a commercial for New Country Corn Flakes. 'American Gothic' now hangs in its permanent home, The Art Institute of Chicago.

What is Homophobia?

Homophobia, from the Greek word *homo*, or abode, is an irrational fear, sometimes even hatred, of owning a home. The causes of homophobia are varied but as a rule involve the worries, usually financial in nature, related to buying and owning a home, as opposed to *renting*. "Despite mortgage rates being at historically low levels, many renters continue to prefer renting over owning," Charles Feldman, the Coldwell Professor of Banking at the Harvard Business School, says. "Typically, the potential homeowner will carefully examine all the associated costs, and benefits, of home ownership; then, after mulling it over and over endlessly in his head for several years, he or she, and his spouse, will jointly decide, sometimes irrationally, to continue to rent." Feldman adds: "Even the generous *mortgage interest deduction* isn't enough to make the homophobic take the plunge and buy." Generally, there are three forms of homophobia: institutionalized homophobia, in which the phobia against buying a home is taboo according to one's upbringing or family values; religious homophobia, in which a priest or rabbi will advise against it as it breaks some archaic religious law; and state-sponsored homophobia, in which a state or municipality may bar private home ownership due to one's gender, color, or credit score.

Friedrich Nietzsche.

What Did Nietzsche Believe?

Friedrich Nietzsche (1844-1900) was a German philosopher, social critic, and humorist. Nietzsche's philosophy is extremely dense and wildly convoluted, and thus almost impossible to understand, even upon close, repeated readings. Some critics have equated understanding Nietzsche with reading a book about celestial mechanics while riding a *roller coaster*. Because of this, plus a highly illegible handwriting indecipherable except under a powerful microscope, for most of his professional life Nietzsche was repeatedly dismissed as a raving lunatic and crackpot. At its core, Nietzsche's philosophy addresses the ability of one to truly understand the essence of things, the importance of questioning all of society's beliefs and dogmas that may historically have been taken as gospel, and the cyclical nature of existence. In *Tod und Verwirrung* ("Death and Confusion", 1894), he wrote:

> *I am at the end nothing, no, less than nothing, a cipher, a crawling insignificant housefly riding the spread wings of an unknowable universal destiny, who can do no wrong or right, except to, properly, view the universe as an existential one, ultimately meaningless, a huge void, black and vacant, dead.*

As the result of a highly contentious working life accompanied by an equally stressful personal one, Nietzsche eventually fell ill, and then went hopelessly insane, possibly from tertiary syphilis. As his life came to a sad, difficult end, Nietzsche was placed in the care of his sister, *Elisabeth*, who tried to push him down a well while riding in his wheelchair.

What Does Passover Celebrate?

Passover is a Jewish festival which celebrates the ancient Israelites speedy exodus from Egypt, in 1450 B.C. at around nine-thirty. The holiday occurs each year just before Easter, when families gather at someone's dining room table to recite prayers in a long-dead language. During this gathering, called a *Seder*, the suffering of the Israelites in Pharaoh's Egypt is recalled, as well as the interminable list of trials and tribulations Jews have suffered throughout history, such as the Spanish Inquisition, the Holocaust, and attending *Hebrew school*. Even though Passover is meant to be a joyous occasion, because of the foregoing many participants, and some invited Gentiles, depart the Seder feeling guilty, even depressed, which is probably the whole point. The most important part of any Seder is the gigantic, highly caloric meal immediately following the prayer service, which usually includes chicken soup, mixed vegetables, red wine, unleavened bread (or matzos), chicken again with some form of sticky translucent glaze on top, culminating in a colorful array of cakes, cookies, and other sugary treats.

What Was the Longest Tennis Match in History?

The longest match in tennis history occurred between August 6 and August 8, 1997, in Brentwood, California. The unusually long contest, between Dr. David Rosen, a Brentwood, California podiatrist, and his close friend, Dr. Melvin Siegel, a Beverly Hills plastic surgeon, was held over three days in broiling 103 degree heat, on Rosen's private court just behind his sprawling ten-acre thirty-bedroom mansion. The match, 52 hours and 39 minutes in length, ended in a draw after both men collapsed suddenly, and had to be transported to Cedars Sinai Medical Center for quintuple bypass surgery. Both men survived, but gave up tennis in favor of long walks and golf.

Is Time Travel Possible?

The concept of travelling backward or forward in time, or jumping between points in space, is, along with the ability to *control* time, most likely impossible. Despite this, many scientists, like Einstein in his *Special Theory of Relativity*, and numerous authors, including Washington Irving as well as H.G. Wells in his famous book, *The Time Machine*, have postulated various creative ways in which time travel could possibly occur. Broadly, however, the problem with time travel, aside from its various accompanying paradoxes, is that it would necessitate an object initially travelling *slower* than light to travel *faster* than light (FTL), a feat requiring not only an infinite amount of energy but also Herculean patience, courage and money. The only known instance of true time travel, is the case of Rip Van Reagan, a Depression-era actor and later TV host, who fell asleep in California, slept for twenty years, then woke up in Washington, D.C., where he had, somehow, become President of the United States.

How Common is Cheating?

Gaining an unfair advantage in a competitive situation by breaking the rules, or *cheating*, has become common throughout American society. Although the practice takes many forms, from insider stock trading to steroid use amongst professional athletes to shacking up with your best friend's wife, cheating in the past several years has swiftly metastasized, reaching into America's once-hallowed educational system, infecting high schools, universities, and even kindergarten classrooms. Instances of cheating by tiny children, some as young as two years old, are now daily occurrences, as ambitious youngsters, prompted by their insatiably wealthy, prestige-hungry parents, vie for increasingly rare openings in big city daycare centers and highly selective private schools. In one instance, an overly aggressive four-year-old seeking special treatment handed an envelope containing ten thousand dollars in fifties to an administrator in charge of admissions. Amongst the college-bound, paying professional test takers to take the SAT so as to gain much higher scores and increase their chances of gaining highly prized slots in the Ivy League, is not uncommon, threatening the entire system. "The Ivy League – it's today's Holy Grail," one educator at an elite boarding school in New Hampshire laments. "Parents will do almost anything, and I mean

53

anything, short of murder of course, to get their kids high test scores so they can get into Harvard, Yale, or Princeton. Even Cornell isn't good enough anymore. It's totally insane out there, and rampant cheating is the result."

Is Nuclear War Likely?

According to a highly classified 2010 report by the RAND Corporation, a U.S. government think tank based in Santa Monica, California, "some kind of nuclear event" in the next twenty years is "probably unavoidable." For this reason, a better question is: "Is nuclear war *survivable?*" Although America and Russia are at peace, with cooperation between the two Cold War foes occurring on a number of different fronts, both countries still maintain tens of thousands of strategic nuclear warheads arrayed against each other, all on hair-trigger "launch-on-warning" alert. For this reason, even a single momentary miscalculation, on either side, could trigger a nuclear exchange that in as little as ten minutes could quickly escalate into *worldwide nuclear war*. If a nuclear war *did* occur – even a "partial" one involving less than fifty hydrogen bombs in the one-megaton range either between the U.S. and Russia, between Russia and China, or between any combination of the world's declared nuclear powers – it would end in sudden, unimaginable catastrophe. According to RAND, in such a scenario all U.S. cities with populations over 100,000 would be reduced within a matter of minutes to the consistency of a charcoal briquette, as would all Russian (and probably Chinese) cities, as well as 100% of both country's defense installations. Massive civilian deaths from blast, heat, and radiation would quickly overwhelm hospitals and health care systems, and all meaningful economic activity on both sides would immediately cease. A *radioactive shroud*, consisting mainly of soot and debris from burning cities, would quickly encircle the globe, blocking out the sun and ending human life as we know it. Despite this, many U.S. politicians, almost all of them conservative Republicans subservient to defense contractors allied with America's vast military-industrial complex, (See: *"What's the 'Military Industrial Complex'?"*) have consistently advocated an even larger, more robust nuclear force than the one currently in place.

What Do Women Find Attractive?

Women are a mixture of emotions, a well-tossed salad of thoughts and feelings, understood by only their mothers, highly trained expensive psychiatrists, and hairdressers. In many cases, women receive their first impressions about a man on the first date. Men should thus be extremely careful about how they conduct themselves during this critical initial meeting. A few basic rules and regulations should always be followed. Men should arrange to meet a woman only in a public well-lit location, between 7:45 and 8:50 p.m., and never on Tuesday. The man should dress conservatively, preferably in a dark suit and matching tie to indicate he's capable (eventually) of becoming a reliable breadwinner, and possibly father. Good grooming cannot be overemphasized: a man's hair should be neat, but not overly so; a small amount of oil is acceptable, but not like a North Sea oil slick. On a first date, a man should at least *appear* to be highly confident, even courageous, but not arrogant or demeaning although a slight amount of arrogance is sometimes called for especially amongst the *professional classes*. He should avoid lisping, stuttering, coughing, and any other distracting behavior that might indicate anxiety, nervousness, tension or doubt. His words should be well-chosen but not oratorical, his voice low but not too low, but not high either – a middle vocal range, such as tenor or contralto, is probably best. A good sense of humor can be highly attractive to a woman, *assuming she has one too*. Following the meal, the male should reach forward casually, pick up the check, and pay *in full*, but only with a valid major credit card and never with cash which could be misinterpreted as indicating poor credit. Most importantly, after any first date a man should always perform sex safely by using a *pre-stressed* ribbed condom with a slight scent.

What's the Worst City in America?

Since 2007, San Bernardino, located 65 miles east of Los Angeles in California's San Bernardino Valley, has held the dubious official title of "America's Worst City". Site of the world's first McDonald's restaurant, the McDonald's Museum, and Norton Air Force Base, named after Art Carney's comic character "Norton" in the long-running CBS TV show *The Honeymooners,* the city boasts 209,000 residents and an average daytime temperature of 118 degrees Fahrenheit. Due to extreme ineptitude plus colossal financial mismanagement, including but not limited to accounting errors, lack of revenue growth, increases in pension costs, lucrative labor agreements, and the state's raid on its redevelopment funds, San Bernardino in July 2012 found itself $46 million in debt and unable to meet its payroll, forcing it to become the third California city in the same month to seek Chapter 9 bankruptcy protection. Making matters worse, city budget officials had falsified documents presented to the mayor and city council for 13 years prior to bankruptcy, masking the city's deficit spending and true debt costs. "Our supposed leaders have wasted tons of money and made our lives potentially even more depressingly horrible and utterly miserable than they already are," one horribly depressed suicidal longtime city resident said. "Show me a bridge, any bridge – I want to jump off it, right now."

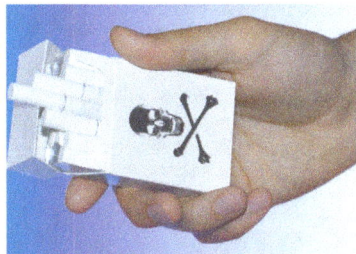

What's the 'Tobacco Lobby'?

The tobacco lobby is a separate area smokers can go into when they don't want to disturb non-smokers by smoking. All restaurants within a 20-mile radius of Akron, Ohio, as well as any hotel or motel with more than 600 rooms with a Q in its name, are required to provide a separate designated area free of the extremely harmful effects of tobacco smoke and its accompanying numerous carcinogens known to cause *cancer*, and eventually certain death. One infamous U.S. District Court case paved the way for a so-called tobacco lobby. In *Hackmeyer v. Eddie's Route 66 Diner*, two longtime smokers hopelessly addicted to cigarettes sued a small roadside restaurant for forcing them to move to the lobby to smoke. Ruling in the case, U.S. Circuit Court Judge Stansfield Coughlin wrote for the majority that "under the sixth, eighth, fifteenth and forty-second amendments, smokers have no rights whatsoever...", and should be immediately sent to prison. In reacting to *Hackmeyer*, Congress passed the *Go Outside and Kill Yourself* Law, mandating that smokers should be accommodated whenever possible but only in certain rare instances where no Congressman over four foot eight is hurt by losing votes, ushering in the term "tobacco lobby".

What's the 'Gun Lobby'?

(See: "*What's the 'Tobacco Lobby'?*")

Who Invented the Hammer?

According to United States Patent Office records, patent application 815,220 for "A force amplifier – a device to drive nails, forge metal and smash things to bits" was submitted on January 13, 1987, by Apple Computer Corporation of Cupertino, California. In rejecting Apple's application, the Patent Office stated: "There is absolutely nothing new, novel, or technically unique about patentee's device…as the exact same instrument, with few variations, has already been in active use for numerous millennia. Application is thus hereby rejected." Notwithstanding Apple's application, and its stated intention to file vigorous patent infringement litigation against "any entity that threatens our exclusive rights in this asset," archeological records clearly show the hammer has been in use since the early Paleolithic Stone Age, around 2,400,000 BCE, and is probably the oldest human tool.

What's the Worst Food to Eat?

Although most foods are nutritious and healthful, some are known to be extremely unhealthy, even *toxic*. According to the U.S. Food and Drug Administration, the most dangerous food a human can eat is Aunt Tillie's (17 oz.) Chicken Pot Pie. At 890 calories, with 19 grams of saturated fat and 1400 mg of sodium, continuous use of the product, even in moderation, can lead to severe health problems, such as obesity, diabetes, and eventually, sudden cardiac arrest. "This is a terrible, almost evil, food," Dr. Milton Cheeseburger, an emergency cardiac surgeon at the Massachusetts General Hospital in Boston, says. "Eating an Aunt Tillie's chicken pie, and other frozen prepared foods like it, is just slightly healthier than downing a gallon bucket of pure lard." He adds: "Despite being increasingly health conscious, Americans' *actual* eating habits, paradoxically, continue to quickly deteriorate. For some unknown reason which defies logic, people still flock to fast food joints like McDonald's, Burger King, and Taco Bell, where death by arteriosclerosis is almost guaranteed – if you keep it up long enough." According to Cheeseburger, at 1220 calories and a whopping 61 g of fat per serving, high on the list of bad *fast* foods is McDonald's Deluxe Breakfast. "It'll clog all your major arteries and stop your heart in less than an hour," he says, almost laughing. "That means it's bad, *real* bad. I'd sooner ingest pure cyanide."

How Accurate is the U.S. Unemployment Rate?

Each month the U.S. Bureau of Labor Statistics divides the number of unemployed workers by the total workforce. The result is called the *unemployment rate*. Government bureaucrats and economists with Ph.D.'s from Princeton know that this *official* rate is wildly unreliable and laughably inaccurate. Despite this, this number is quickly disseminated to the media, and is used to judge whether a president is doing his job properly, or just giving lip service to America's vast ocean of unemployed, many of whom would kill a close relative just to get a minimum-wage job at a corner gas station. The unemployment rate has been criticized in recent years as seriously understating true unemployment by excluding many people. A more accurate figure would include all workers currently looking for work, who looked for a while then stopped, who thought about looking for work for a few hours but never did, those at home who are depressed and about to kill themselves, and those who have a job but one so low-paying and demeaning they prefer *not* to report that they even have it.

Where Does Queen Elizabeth Live?

Queen Elizabeth II ascended the British throne in 1952. She is the Head of the Commonwealth of realms and also the Church of England. Queen Elizabeth is a nice lady who smiles a lot, wears big hats, and spends much of her time riding in a carriage with her husband Prince Philip and doing charity work. Not much is known about the Queen personally as she never gives interviews. With a personal net worth estimated at 450 million pounds, the Queen is very rich but not anywhere near as rich as Warren Buffet or even Mark Zuckerberg. The Queen's hobbies include equestrianism, collecting Welsh corgi dogs, and carrying her purse. The Queen lives officially in London at One Buckingham Palace SW1, but also spends time at Balmoral Castle and Sandringham Castle, but not *too* much time as they're very big, drafty and cold, especially in February. She also occasionally sleeps in the *Duchy of Lancaster*, 46,000 acres of farmland and historic buildings owned by the Queen, located in various parts of England and Wales. Queen Elizabeth does not work, but since the Norman Invasion in 1066 has received an unemployment check in the form of a generous stipend from Her Majesty's Treasury to cover all expenses related to her official duties. The anti-monarchy group *Republic*, which advocates abolishing the Monarchy (but not the Queen herself) estimates maintaining the royal household costs the British people 150 million pounds annually, including security, lost revenue, and mowing the lawn.

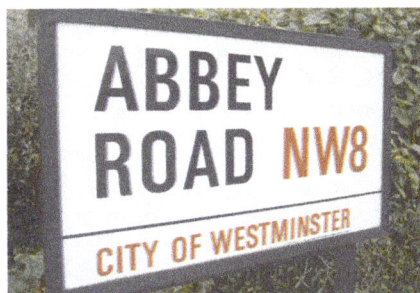

Who Was the 'Fifth Beatle'?

The Beatles were the most popular and successful pop band in music history. Comprising four members, John Lennon, Paul McCartney, George Harrison, and Ringo Starr, almost from the band's founding in Liverpool in the late 1950's there had been talk of a "fifth Beatle". Although who could legitimately claim the right to the title of fifth Beatle has constantly been debated, there's never been a clear answer, or even consensus. McCartney himself has always insisted the fifth Beatle was Brian Epstein, the group's manager from 1961 to 1967; others disagreed, saying that George Martin, the producer and often arranger of almost all the Beatles' early hits, was the fifth. In the early 1980's, people claiming to be the *sixth* Beatle began to appear as well. These included, among many others, John Sixcliffe, a London window washer who claims to have "witnessed" all of the Beatles' major recording sessions while washing windows at the Beatles' EMI recording facilities in London; and Reggie Dalrymple, a Liverpool cab driver who said it was *he* who regularly "drove the lads around back home" long before they became famous. Still others have claimed to be the seventh, eighth, and even fourteenth Beatle, including Mona McFall, a London seamstress who once darned a sock for John Lennon, and Ron "Buzzy" Davis, a New York handyman who replaced a light bulb in the Fab Four's dressing room just prior to their historic February 1964 appearance on the Ed Sullivan Show.

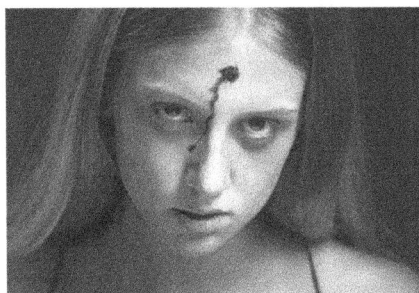

Is There Life After Death?

Throughout history people have conjectured whether there is life after death, or an *afterlife*. The answer to the possibility of an afterlife varies widely from religion to religion. The Sadducees, for example, an ancient Jewish sect, believed in a god, but no afterlife. Buddhists, on the other hand, generally believe in an afterlife, but no god. In most religions, however, the common concept of an existence after death is that an individual dies, is re-born on earth, then begins the cycle all over again as, for example, an insect, a snake, or a bank president, without any knowledge of a prior existence. In modern times, through extensive experimentation and empirical observation, scientists have been able to determine that life after death is an almost 100% certainty. Hubert Coffin-Sloan, Emeritus Professor of Religion at MIT, says that "undeniable proof of life after death" is all around us, every day. "Go to a funeral, any funeral, and you'll see people standing around – crying, gossiping, eating," Coffin-Sloan says. "Someone near and dear to them has passed away, but they're completely alive, proving there's life after death." The opposite of the idea of an afterlife is *eternal oblivion*, or *nothingness*, where a person dies and is then permanently unconscious, a state some have compared to watching daytime TV, or doing the laundry.

How Important is a Good Resume?

In today's extremely competitive job market, the importance of a clearly-presented coherent resume cannot be overemphasized. A resume is a calling-card, the very first thing a prospective employer sees, and if it's bad or clunky, there's little chance of gaining even an *interview*, let alone a job offer. Although all industries and professions are different, several guidelines should be strictly adhered to: First, a resume should be printed on *plain white paper*, and be clear of smudges, spots, food stains or misspellings which could be distracting and usually indicate sloppiness and a lack of genuine interest. Keep a resume *as short as possible*, and in no event longer than sixteen pages. A lengthy long-winded resume is an immediate turnoff as well as a tip-off indicating extreme arrogance, boorishness, and even deep-seeded psychological problems. A resume should be *highly focused:* never be vague in your "Career Objective" by saying something bland and clichéd like, for example: "Candidate's objective is to see new people and places, and to make lots of money while helping to establish permanent peace throughout the world." Always make sure your resume, at least in some tangential way, *fits the job description.* Don't apply to work on the newest app (See: *"What is an App?"*) at your favorite software company if your resume indicates you've been laboring in a Tennessee coal mine for the last ten years. Finally, always always always *follow up*, preferably within as little as a few hours but never longer than two years. You may be absolutely perfect for a position, your credentials outshining everyone else's on the planet, but if you submit a sterling resume and then immediately take a four-month holiday in Botswana without following its progress, you're almost guaranteed to never get a job offer. The squeaky wheel *very often* gets the grease.

Why is There So Much Divorce?

Statistics, unfortunately, almost never lie. And the statistics indicate that half of all marriages in the U.S. end in divorce within one year, leaving acrimony, loneliness, poverty, plus a giant collection of broken homes and ex-spouse's framed portraits, in their wakes. Although the exact reasons for the so-called "epidemic of divorce" have been endlessly written about and hotly debated, the primary culprits seem to be clearer every passing year: (1) overly high expectations, leading to almost hilariously predictable dissatisfaction; (2) the extreme relative mobility of young people, especially in America, allowing couples to end a bad marriage easily, quickly, and cleanly; and (3) rampant, almost laughable carelessness on the part of people when choosing a mate. Many men and women fall in love, and then marry on impulse and usually for the wrong reasons, a sad scenario often culminating in divorce. Fortunately, in the not too distant future all marriages will be arranged using a gigantic array of powerful interconnected supercomputers, eliminating all the guesswork and guaranteeing an almost 100% success rate.

Is Smoking in Bed Dangerous?

Smoking in bed is extremely hazardous. Although the Great Fire of London in 1666 started in a bakery, another disaster, the *Huge Conflagration of 1818*, began when ashes from a sleeping man's cigar dropped onto his bedclothes, leading to the destruction of half of Havana, Cuba. The U.S. Sleep Safety Council, a non-profit 401 (c) (6) organization devoted to non-profit sleep safety, advises smoking only in designated areas of the home, especially in April. The following is the Sleep Safety Council's *"Seven Things You Should Never Do"*, a list updated annually:

- Never smoke in, under, over, or in the general vicinity of your bed.

- Never use a candle in or near your bed. Miniature incandescent bulbs were first commercially available in 1878, so try to use one of those instead.

- Never use candles or matches while small children are in bed with you. Children are not sophisticated enough to know the dangers of being in bed with a candle, matches, or a stupid adult.

- Never use a space heater in any bed, even a king sized one. Keep the space heater on the floor and follow the instructions.

- Don't run electrical wires into your bed, then around your upper body and legs ten times, to keep warm. That's what electric blankets are for.

- Never drink any liquid (except wine in moderation) in bed while using a space heater or electric blanket. Water may drip down onto the blanket, and deep cook you like fried chicken or toasted ravioli.

- Always dispose of the plastic wrapping that came with your mattress before smoking in bed. Plastic is extremely flammable and can cause immediate death if left unattended.

Who was the Best President?

The general consensus amongst historians is that best president in U.S. history was Millard Fillmore. The precise reasons for this, however, are mostly unknown. One *possible* reason is that, unlike modern presidents, Fillmore throughout his life studiously avoided the limelight, and tried to remain, sometimes obsessively so, as inconspicuous as possible, even as president. The country's 13th president, Fillmore was born in upstate New York near Buffalo, the second of nine children. After learning cloth-making and agreeing to marry his first love Abigail Powers in 1826, he accepted an invitation to enter the bar with a close friend who would later become Postmaster General. In 1828, despite dropping out of sight for three months, Fillmore was elected to the New York State Assembly on the anti-Masonic ticket, where he was enlisted to help enact a new bankruptcy law. Following his mentor, Thurlow Weed, into Congress in1832, Fillmore lost a bid to become Speaker of the House after staying in bed for six weeks. Fillmore's *Tariff of 1842*, a bill to reverse the Compromise Tariff of 1833, was vetoed by President John Tyler. After a disastrous bid to become Governor of New York, Fillmore narrowly defeated Orville Hungerford to become State Comptroller. In 1848, Fillmore was tapped to become Zachary Taylor's running mate, a move designed to block his onetime mentor Thurlow

Weed from obtaining it. As Vice-President, Fillmore favored slavery in several states; and during congressional debates over The Compromise of 1850, in which Senator Henry Foote of Mississippi famously pulled a pistol on Senator Thomas Hart Benton of Missouri, *Fillmore remained silent.* After Zachary Taylor's sudden death in 1850, Fillmore became president. Fillmore's entire cabinet resigned, however, when Fillmore refused to block the *Fugitive Slave Act,* in which federal marshals were required to arrest runaway slaves or risk a substantial fine. Fillmore is best remembered by historians for resolving a dispute with Portugal, and smoothing over a disagreement with Peru. Fillmore will also be well-remembered, or forgotten, for being the first president without substantial personal wealth, and who spent most of his career antagonizing as few people as possible, most of them historians, by remaining as *anonymous* as possible.

What is an App?

An app, short for *application,* is a type of computer software specifically designed to perform a function or task, or a series of related tasks. App software differs from *operating software* in that it is generally not related to the internal functioning of a computer, but operates as an "add-on". For this reason, apps are sometimes very powerful as they are only being asked to work on, or solve, a very specific task at any one time. Apps are usually designed by computer geeks, or *nerds,* some as young as ten, in the high-tech area around Silicon Valley in California, as well by other "developers" in many cities throughout the world. In recent years, the popularity of apps has exploded, so there are literally hundreds of thousands of them, possibly millions, and have thus become highly specific, some would even say *unnecessary.* For example, one app is able to immediately locate and open all electric garage doors within a five-mile radius of the user. Another app, developed by two teens in Menlo Park, California, allows the user to accurately calculate the number of single "highly promiscuous" women within a shopping mall who have a sister but no current boyfriend, *and pinpoint their location.*

79

Is Mideast Peace Possible?

Peace in the Middle East is possible, and *already exists* in many places today: Jordan is at peace with Saudi Arabia, Egypt is at peace with Lebanon, Lebanon is at peace with Jordan, and Syria is at peace with Egypt. The lone remaining holdouts are Israel and the Palestinians – the reasons complex. Essentially, the Palestinians profoundly resent having to live simultaneously in a sardine can by the sea called the Gaza Strip and in a golf trap called the West Bank, while the Israelis are annoyed that their cities get rocketed occasionally by kids in the Gaza Strip where every day is the Fourth of July. Despite the ongoing enmity between the two sides which has lasted for millennia (due mainly to a lack of capable translators), some broad-minded citizens have decided to bypass the bickering governments involved and make peace directly. Near Hebron, a shepherd named Mohammad regularly eats lunch, then plays canasta with, his Jewish friend Avi; and two high-schoolers near Betar Illit, one a Jew and the other a Palestinian, have invented an app together (See: *"What is an App?"*) that locates like-minded peace-loving teens within a ten-mile radius who like *Deep Purple.*

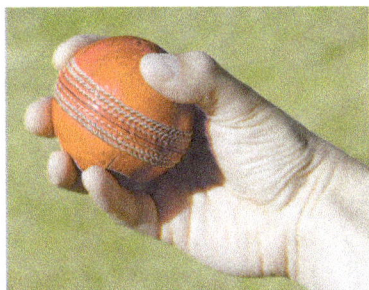

How is Cricket Played?

Cricket is a game played in England and India, usually on sunny days in a park or field, with two days off between games for air travel. Invented in 16th century England by Jiminy Cricket, the game is very similar to American baseball in that one team wins and the other loses. Each team, or *side*, consists of eleven men, or humans, who try to hit a round red or white ball as far as they can while standing dangerously close to a target, or *wicket*. If the ball is pitched, or *bowled*, and hits the wicket or is caught, the player batting is shot by firing squad or immediately deported, whichever comes first. Other features of the game including fielding, dismissals, extras, team structure and ticket prices are wildly convoluted and generally understood only by mathematics dons at Cambridge and Oxford. As a result, cricket has lost many fans who otherwise would be if they understood what they were watching.

About the Author

Marc Berlin is an author, actor, filmmaker, and satirist. When not writing, he takes long walks in the woods and cranberry bogs near his home in eastern Massachusetts. His website is at *www.marcberlin.net.*

Also by Marc Berlin

That Cloud Looks Like Jesus

www.ingramcontent.com/pod-product-compliance
Lightning Source LLC
LaVergne TN
LVHW022325080426

835508LV00013BA/1323

* 9 7 8 0 9 8 5 9 6 2 4 2 5 *